The Key is Alignment

DEFINING AUTHENTICITY ~ DEVELOPING INTUITION ~ ATTRACTING YOUR DESIRES

CRISTINA M LINDSAY

BALBOA.PRESS
A DIVISION OF HAY HOUSE

Balboa Press books may be ordered through booksellers or by contacting:

Balboa Press
A Division of Hay House
1663 Liberty Drive
Bloomington, IN 47403
www.balboapress.com
1 (877) 407-4847

Because of the dynamic nature of the Internet, any web addresses or
links contained in this book may have changed since publication and
may no longer be valid. The views expressed in this work are solely those
of the author and do not necessarily reflect the views of the publisher,
and the publisher hereby disclaims any responsibility for them.

The author of this book does not dispense medical advice or prescribe the use
of any technique as a form of treatment for physical, emotional, or medical
problems without the advice of a physician, either directly or indirectly. The
intent of the author is only to offer information of a general nature to help
you in your quest for emotional and spiritual well-being. In the event you use
any of the information in this book for yourself, which is your constitutional
right, the author and the publisher assume no responsibility for your actions.

Illustrations by Carmen M. Lindsay

Print information available on the last page.

ISBN: 978-1-9822-4560-3 (sc)
ISBN: 978-1-9822-4562-7 (hc)
ISBN: 978-1-9822-4561-0 (e)

Library of Congress Control Number: 2020905890

Balboa Press rev. date: 06/27/2020

For my parents who encouraged me for my entire life to write a book . . . this one's for you mom and dad, I love and miss you every day!

TABLE OF CONTENTS

INTRODUCTION

We've all heard the sayings, "trust your intuition" and "listen to your gut feeling", but what exactly *is* intuition? How do we define it? How does it show up for us personally? What if we could more clearly understand the information that intuition is giving us, trust it, and utilize it to make better life choices?

The Google dictionary defines intuition as:

"The ability to understand something immediately, without the need for conscious reasoning. A thing that one knows or considers likely from instinctive feeling rather than conscious reasoning"

Synonyms include: *a hunch, feeling, inkling, suspicion, and impression* . . . just to name a few.

Have you ever had a nagging *feeling* or an awareness of *something*? Have you experienced "red flags" or had a confident *knowing* about a person or situation? This is your intuition communicating with you. Intuition can sometimes be vague (hard to *hear*) or not so vague (screaming at you). It is mental, physical, emotional, and energetic. It is one of our greatest gifts if we can build an understanding and relationship with it. Intuition is innate, we are born with it. It is internal and somehow external at the same time. Intuition is like receiving a radio signal that can alert us or comfort us, and can *definitely* communicate with us. I think we more easily recognize these *signals* when we don't listen to them. We say things like "I knew it, my gut feeling was telling me but I did not listen" or can feel blindsided, like "what the heck just happened?" When in retrospect, the signs were there all along! You know what they say about hindsight being 20/20 . . . who *are they* anyways??

We all have intuition; it is instinctual. We are hard-wired with it. We have all experienced it. My intent is to help you *develop* this instinct and offer you tools to more clearly define it for yourself as an individual. For each of us, this "sixth sense" is unique, no different than your thumbprint, your eye color, or your preferences. Intuition can be less in the forefront from your other senses of sight, smell, touch, hearing, and taste but no less present and vital to how you experience life.

My journey of writing this book speaks from the defining moments in my life where intuition has been the common denominator. More accurately, when I did NOT listen to it and made decisions that were to be my life lessons, and ultimately information I now *feel* compelled to share with you. I had no idea that I was going to write about intuition. My writing began as a journal about feeling completely lost in my life. I had been on a very clear path and then suddenly found myself in the wilderness with no map and no provisions . . . the only thing I could do is to keep going and learn to fine tune my instincts and my intuition in order to find my way back to my Self once more. I started journaling about that particular experience now titled "LOST" and then kept writing about all of the past major life events that had strongly affected my life . . . all the way back to childhood. I began to recognize a pattern. It was one of those "a-ha!"(or more like an "oh shit!") moments when I realized that this pattern had played out again and again in my most impactful life experiences. The underlying lesson in each experience was my lack of listening to and trusting my intuition. There it was . . . clear as day. It was devastating and embarrassing. Why had I not seen this before? I was filled with regret and resentment towards myself. I wanted to look away and ignore it, stay in a space of unawareness, and pretend it was not there . . . but I couldn't. Every fiber in my body, every thought, and every feeling was shouting in my ear. There was no escaping this life lesson. I could choose to face it or be destined to repeat it again. I knew I was being asked to walk through this wilderness, into a landscape completely unfamiliar and learn to *really* trust my relationship with something larger than myself (yet connected somehow) for maybe the very first time in my life. I had to learn to holistically develop and trust my intuition. It was like a friend of mine often says, "I was hit by a spiritual 2x4!" Sometimes things have to completely get torn apart in order to rebuild them stronger and more intentionally designed. It can seriously suck at the time but I promise that if you go through the process, it WILL pay off.

What if we could demystify intuition, learn to recognize it more clearly, and build our self-confidence by learning to trust it? That is exactly what we are about to do. In this book, you will discover new patterns of decision making that better serve your life. You will learn about *who you really are* and *what you really want*! You will learn about the guiding information that is available to help you at all times. You will learn to get a bird's eye view of any situation and gain very clear signals about what decisions to make. You will gain skills that will help attract your heart's desires into your life. Most of all, you will learn what it takes to feel completely "comfortable in your own skin" and live a happier life!

I invite you to come with me on this journey. In truth, this is a journey we are all on together! We are on an exploration in search of authenticity and confident life choices. Life is all about defining your true self by intuitively remembering *who you really are* and fully stepping into it. By developing your intuition, you can make better decisions and gain clarity within every situation. This allows you to stay true to your authentic self and not be sidetracked away from your goals and your desires. This is *your life* and you are the co-creator in the direction of your life and how you choose to live it. It's never too late to live the life your heart desires. Let's get started!

CHAPTER 1
LOST

We've all been there; maybe you are there now, LOST. Or for me more accurately . . . LOST AGAIN, the sequel.

Lost is a strange place. A land filled with uncomfortable feelings of uncertainty, vulnerability, and a sense of being untethered. One day it seems the path is clear, you have a plan, and you're chuggin' along and then, all of the sudden . . . the path is gone, vanished. It led you into an unfamiliar territory or it just plain stops and you find yourself wondering what happened? What happened to my passion? What happened to my commitment to my plan? Why isn't this working? What do I do next? What do I want now?

For many of us, this place can be debilitating, confusing, and depressing. So we begin to analyze the situation and search for options. We make lists of pros and cons but our hearts and spirits feel diminished, our energy is low, so we keep *thinking* our way through. We formulate a new plan, start a new hobby, get a new haircut, or begin a new diet . . . anything that *feels* new. We try to unstick ourselves in many ways, *outward* ways. We try to anesthetize our feelings. We drink alcohol, do drugs, over-eat, binge watch TV, anything to numb ourselves in order to not face the challenges. Often times with the same result . . . LOST.

The most recent chapter in my life story that falls into the category of LOST began after working at a thirty-three year career of owning and operating my business. I loved my customers and did not hate my job . . . I just felt like I was living an automated life . . . I did not feel as though I was really enjoying my life. My spirit felt an un-named longing. I had a feeling of emotional "flatness" and recognized the fact that weeks were quickly turning into months and months turning into years. I had hit the wall of routine and found myself in a rut.

Now if you know me, my *mind* loves to explore these confusing places and look to *create* change in my life, so I jumped right in, no surprise to the people close to me! I have often been told that I "think too much" or spend too much time with "my head in the clouds". You know, I am the one labeled the "dreamer" or "Pollyanna" of this world usually with and eye roll and a sigh or two. The rebellious side of me wants to take on that challenge and prove all of those judgements to be wrong!

Challenge accepted. Hooked again.

So I started to make lists (oh yeah, I am a list person too). The catalyst for this particular exploration had sparked from a recent conversation with a dear friend who asked me "what makes me happy?" HAPPY?? What the heck is that? It really bothered me that I could not clearly answer. I could tell you what made me feel content, fulfilled, safe, secure . . . but happy? A simple and provocative question. I did not have a clear, concise answer and truth be told, I'm still working on it years later.

I began to seek out books and articles written about happiness but it was like reading a generic story. They did not resonate with my spirit or my heart. Happiness resides in those places. I longed to *feel* happy. It was in that moment, I realized that I was not really *feeling* my emotions. I could describe some levels of emotion that satisfied my mind but was not *really connecting* to my heart or my spirit. I made the decision to try a new practice of *feeling* my way through this search for happiness and then utilizing my mind for the words, for the list, and for the plan. I wanted to use my *feelings* as the light that illuminates the path. I longed for a sense of being *drawn to* something in life versus being *driven to*. The heartfelt pull of "I want to" instead of the mindset of "I have/need to or should". I began searching for a more holistic approach on how to make decisions based on *feelings* instead of just thoughts. Of course, this can be kind of murky at times as feelings can be tricky things. But I was determined to do it differently. I was living a "flat" emotional life, not able to access *feelings*. I was "gun shy" about trusting my mind to come up with another new plan. What's the definition of insanity? "Doing the same thing over and over and expecting different results". I felt like my compass was wrong, broken somehow. I had been relying on my mind for most of my life, always hatching up new ideas and charting my course. Anyone who knows me well can attest to that! I had made my *mind* my "true north". I had forgotten about heart based feelings and accessing intuition. I had the realization that the way I had been operating was not providing me the *quality* of life I longed for, I was not happy. I recognized that I wanted and needed to develop different areas of myself, learn to trust my gut . . . letting go of the illusion of control and *allowing* life to lead me instead of the other way around . . . me leading life. It *felt* risky and it *felt* right.

I began with trying to define the qualities of happiness. What is required for happiness to exist? Here is what I discovered. For me, to experience *feelings* of happiness, it requires: good physical health, a balance of creativity and productivity, being in nature, emotional and mental connections with others, and a strong sense of abundance and gratitude. The result of these is *feeling happy*. Happiness itself, *feels* relaxed, light, and holds an air of optimism and openness. You see, this is an "inside" job. This was not about looking to external factors to determine my happiness. Happiness was not necessarily a new job, a new place, a new outfit, or a new (fill in the blank). This exploration is about defining your *internal* compass to measure those external factors against to see if they fit the bill. Each of us has our own compass to recalibrate and dis-cover by asking some simple but powerful questions. In my experience, exploring this question of "what is required to *feel* happiness in my life?" has (and still is), taken me years to discern and refine. It's helpful to revisit this question on occasion because the answers can shift, change, and become clear with time and experience as a result of the different seasons in our lives. What was important to my happiness in my twenties could be different in my fifties, even though some aspects are the same and consistent.

This then led me to the *external* question of "what is fun?" because fun and happiness seem to be linked . . . baffling. No friggin' idea. I have had a life of working, being responsible, and living paycheck to paycheck. I was a single mom for ten years; I have worked fulltime since I was fifteen years old and owned my own business from the age of twenty-three. Fun? Not so much. Maybe in moments, definitely with people. Don't get me wrong, all of those things have given me a sense of fulfillment, accomplishment, and joy. They taught me responsibility, independence, and the importance of integrity . . . but fun? I could not pin that one down. Society and media show us images of fun, like playing sports, picnics in the park, and vacations. Those realities seemed out of reach for me. I was getting by. I was ok. Just ok.

I paid my bills, got my daughter to school and skating lessons, cooked dinners for my family, and made sure my coworkers had a place to make a living (including myself). But I did not see myself picnicking with friends or riding my bike through the park with the sun shining or going on exotic cruises wearing the perfect white sundress . . . all of the external ideas that those images provoke as a definition of fun.

I put that one aside for a while. I thought if I made more money, I could *afford* fun. Yup, I went down *that* rabbit hole. We all know where it led . . . decades later . . . a bigger house, a better location for the business, a newer car . . . more debt. My daughter now grown but still financially needing help from my husband and I (we had gotten married when she was ten years old), caring, and I mean *day to day caring* for aging parents now living with me, **CANCER** (another enlightening adventure) . . . now in my fifties asking myself those same questions again! SERIOUSLY?

And yes . . . seriously. This time, with pencil in hand, a fresh new legal pad, and twenty more years of life experience of learning what I *don't* want. I continue to find clarity on the answers to these questions. What makes me happy? What is fun?

And then suddenly, out of the blue . . . a *huge* opportunity came along. We had the opportunity to *completely* change our lives. It was a gift. It seemed to fit the bill. It checked off the items on my list of what I had defined was happiness and (hopefully) fun. All of our hard work and determination offered this reward! Our spirits were renewed, we felt like we had a new start and a breath of fresh air. We had a DREAM. It was a new and exciting chapter in our lives and in our marriage . . . finally, our time had arrived!

It meant selling our home, seriously downsizing, moving across country, leaving our careers, learning a new business, and being together. We were "all in". It was an opportunity that felt like we were turning a corner from a season of life that had been filled with challenges to a time of reaping our rewards!

Through all of these years, my husband and I had worked in the day-to-day business of life on the "hamster wheel". You know what I'm talking about. Get up and work ten to twelve hours a day, come home, eat, do what needs to be done, go to bed, get up, and do it again . . . six days a week. Not a lot of fun, no time or energy for friends and family, no time or energy for hobbies and interests. We were tired . . . mentally, physically, emotionally, and spiritually. We were the walking dead . . . we were not *living*.

We said YES to the dream!!

With this opportunity for a new life, we begin to hatch our NEW LIFE PLAN. This process was over a two year span of preparation, getting our home ready to sell, making decisions and strategies for our new business, and figuring out where we will live once we get there. It's a wonderful experience to *feel* the endorphins and adrenaline that comes with newness, like being newly "in love". Can you remember those feelings? Who needs sleep?? Who cares what's for dinner?? Your heart is full, you smile a lot more, and your mind is racing in a good way. It had been so long since that excitement was present and the greatest gift was that we were doing this together, as a team . . . it was a little scary but mostly exhilarating! So off we went!

We put our house on the market with the belief that it would sell in a flash, it didn't . . . <u>another year went by</u>, no sale. We took it off the market confused, frustrated, and discouraged. I questioned the situation for the first time at this point. Was God trying to tell me something? Was this a red flag? I was not sure about how to read this. I leaned onto the idea that this was a "not now" instead of a "no". So we decided to re-group and re-plan. We were so emotionally and physically tired at this point but the promise of being released from our current situation willed us on. In retrospect, I recognize that our determination muscles were tired but strong. Looking back, there were many times that we would question each other about if we were meant to do this or even still wanted to do this and, to be honest in this moment, I had some reservations but my *mind* (and other people) told me it was all part of the process of change, especially a BIG one. My *feelings* told me differently. I labeled them as FEAR . . . and I ignored them.

So we put our house back on the market and it sold in eleven days! There was my sign . . . it was all good. Now, with the flurry of actions that happen when you sell or buy a home, we were in FULL SPEED AHEAD mode. The reality of the dream was finally here! Now the *word* YES went into the *action* of YES. Even writing about it now makes my head spin.

There were many super good aspects about this move for us. After a really challenging decade of caring for my parents (my mom had Alzheimer's and dad had heart disease, now both passed over) and me, going through cancer treatments and surgeries, we finally felt FREE to have this brand new chapter in our lives. It was a new lease on life, a fresh start, and a new beginning. For me, it was the first time in my adult life that I was not responsible for anyone else. The decade before was also hard on our relationship but we endured. We held onto our values about taking care of our parents. It was the "right" thing to do for us . . . not so easy at times, but still the right choice. We would do it all again if we needed to. With this new life ahead of us, we felt like this was the reward for all of the hard work we had put in up until now, the Willy Wonka Golden Ticket. This would allow us to pay off everything and have a new beginning in all areas of life. We could create what comes next, our home, our business, our relationship, and our finances, a clean slate.

So off we went with all of the emotions one faces when starting a new journey into the wilderness, the unknown, a new territory. I now recognize the qualities of vulnerability and courage it takes to say YES to a dream. The excitement and adrenaline in the beginning are intoxicating and when that starts to settle, once more the feelings of fear, doubt, and anxiety eventually surfaced and I found myself questioning my choices again but I still pushed those feelings aside. I put them under the category of change, telling myself that changes this big are going to bring up these feelings and I need to learn how to sit within their rooms of my mind and spend time with them, get to know them, and look them straight in the eye. **I did not do that** . . . nope . . .

too busy . . . I put them into the box marked CHANGE and packed them up onto the moving truck.

We started our journey across country. Along the way, I was feeling the "break away" from our old life and the birthing process into our new life. The anticipation and excitement were palpable. We were doing this . . . *really*. My heart felt full. The chains that shackled me to my former life were broken. I *felt* free. I don't think I had felt this way since I was a kid. It was like riding your bike with no hands, the breeze in your face, confident, and free. I *remembered* the feeling but could not tell you exactly the last time I had felt it. It is a very good feeling!

Much like the birthing process, when we arrived, it felt surreal. Reminds me of getting to the hospital on the day my daughter was born. This is really happening NOW yet it felt like being in a dreamlike state at the same time. It was a bit overwhelming to grasp the reality of the situation, but we dug in our heels and started the process of planting roots into the soil of our new lives.

With a good deal of unfortunate events and over a period of time . . . very very sadly . . . Turns out; it was *not* how I had imagined it. Some of the circumstances of our new life did not welcome us in the way I thought they would. The dream had a cloud over it; it was covered in fog and unable to see. It was as if someone just turned out the light, suddenly flipped the switch and left me completely in the dark. I was completely LOST! What was happening right now??? My mind was spinning out of control, my heart was physically aching . . . how could this happen?? We had left everything . . . our family, our careers, and our home of many years. I told myself about a million times that all of these feelings of un-certainty, un-comfortableness, and un-groundedness were all part of this process, all a part of a big transition. I rationalized. I prayed. I did not understand. A lot comes up when you are face to face with **fear**. Face to face with **truth**. I keep praying for strength and guidance. I cried a lot.

I spent the next months (and sometimes to this very day) going through this uncertain time of not only trying to find my path but simply trying to find the ground! I felt untethered, like the feeling of falling. It was one of the most challenging situations I had been in . . . and that is saying a lot!

Yes, I was face to face with **fear**, face to face with **truth**. Did I make a mistake by saying yes to this dream? Were there signs along the way that I had missed? How did I end up here?

The hard parts to these questions were that the answers appeared to be a big fat YES . . . I did this, I had made a **big fat mistake**. I had ignored my intuition, I seemingly had developed amnesia from all of the lessons I had learned from my past experiences. I had packed up all of the red flags into the change box and moved them with across country with me. I began to grieve. Not necessarily grieving the life I had left behind, more like grieving the fact that I did not pay attention to the signs, the subtle *feelings* that showed up along the way. I felt confused and upset with myself that I had fallen into an old pattern of allowing my *mind* to make all of the decisions once again. Ignoring all of the other intuitive signs, not listening to or more accurately not trusting what my *feelings* were trying to tell me.

Grieving is a confusing, mixed up mess. Like a ball of yarn that's in a knot. It's hard to tell what feelings are coming from where. My emotions were hard to pin down. One minute I felt like "I'm ok, this new life will be ok", and I could exhale. The next minute I was crying for no apparent reason, feeling hopelessness and deep despair. Then I'd find the ground again and start the slow climb back up to my feet once more. Lather, rinse, and repeat . . . again and again. It was mentally and emotionally tiring. I felt more spiritually tested than ever before and truth be told, I'm still there now at times with maybe a little more time on my feet in between the waves of this crazy reality.

But through this cycle, this chapter of LOST . . . I have been able to mine some gold. I have learned so much about myself, my wants, my needs, my beliefs, my boundaries, and my voice. It is hard to see the gifts in the dark, low places but when you find yourself there, if you can muster up enough courage to go inward, sit for a while, look around, and start to notice the small (or not so small) clues . . . you will emerge with new self-knowledge and a stronger spirit. The very things I had previously put aside, the red flags I had ignored and packed into that moving box were the most uncomfortable lessons I needed to look at. I knew it. It was undeniable at this point. Every fiber in my mind, body, and spirit wanted to RUN. Flee the situation, find a new path or more accurately . . . create one. The "flight" part of fight or flight was alive and well, but I stayed for a while, I had to stay and look at myself and look for the **truth** of the situation . . . I chose to sit in this uncomfortable place of uncertainty. My heart literally hurt, my spirit was low and sad, and my body ached as a result. I felt diminished, embarrassed, and foolish. I mentally, emotionally, and spiritually beat myself up. I shamed myself . . . so I sat longer . . . to allow *those* feelings to be there, to let them teach me . . . and they did.

Some of the lessons I learned have offered clarity around my beliefs, what's important to me, what is not, what I am interested in, what moves my heart and spirit, and more easily recognizable, what does NOT! I think for most of us, the latter is so much easier to see and *feel*. We often recognize negative feelings because they are *so* present but they can lead us to their opposites. Pointing out the "no" in order to see the "yes". Our minds can create thoughts that run all over the place. It can weave together stories about a situation that may or may not be true but our *feelings*, our deep down in the gut feelings, can be a more accurate compass if we can peel away the stories and get honest with ourselves.

So during this difficult time, I started a daily journal of what I was *feeling*, not my story, not the actual situation, and especially not what I was thinking! This journal became a new practice of connecting to my feelings and expressing them, gaining clarity, and shining a light into those dark places. I began asking the questions: How do I *feel* physically, emotionally, spiritually, mentally? What am I to learn from this *feeling?* I believe that every situation in life has something to teach us . . . even the "bad" ones. For me, it's been especially the "bad" ones. The struggles, the diagnosis, the unexpected deaths. Those are the big ones. Harder to catch are the smaller, insidious ones. That *little* feeling that something in the situation is not right. The uncomfortable gut feeling that is not obvious and cannot be explained. Being LOST has taught me to pay closer attention to those. It's like a traffic light turned yellow telling me to SLOW DOWN and get ready to STOP, take a minute or two to make sure that I am safe. Make sure there is no oncoming traffic that's going to broadside me, rear end me, or even worse . . . total my life!

When I look back within my own situation of the DREAM, I had many of those small moments that I either ignored completely, explained away or whatever. I simply did not want my dream, my new life, to be destroyed. I grasped onto it because I thought it would take me out of a life that I so desperately wanted to change. And IT DID! Not that the entire DREAM turned out to be negative but in retrospect I would have set it up differently. That was not my path. My path was to experience this uncomfortable and uncertain place so I could learn about myself.

I still get lost to this very day but I am more comfortable than I was. It's a discipline and a practice to get comfortable with being uncomfortable. During this time, I wanted to crawl back out towards the sunshine, find that comfort again, and continue with my life. I had the choice to either stay on this path with my newfound knowledge or choose another path.

I tried to do a combination of both! I decided that I would stay on the DREAM path *and* try to find some familiar grounding by going back into my previous industry in some new way. Back into my comfort zone. I longed to get away from this feeling of living on shaky ground. My mind really wanted to settle in and settle down. I wanted the things on my "happy" list: fun, emotional stability and connection, and abundance. I had put together a resume for the first time in my life since I have been self-employed for my entire career and got out there thinking someone would look at this amazing person and snatch me up! Guess what? That did not happen . . . I got nothing, no responses . . . back into the mucky world of uncomfortable once more. Now I was even more scared than before. I felt I could return to my previous career at any time but . . . apparently not. Obstacles to *my* plan now sent me into a feeling of "free fall". I had jumped out of my comfortable (unhappy) life, now free falling without certainty of where and how I will reach the ground again. It will be in a new place for sure. Will it be a smooth landing? Will I tumble and break a limb? Will I crash and die? Or will I land on my feet? I had better pay attention . . .

So I *am* paying attention, paying attention to *my whole self* and not just my thoughts. Paying attention to the signs and learning to TRUST that I am being directed somehow. All of the non-responses of my job searches, I *feel*, are signs that I am not supposed to be going in that direction at this time. I put it out there and let it go. Now I have learned through past experiences that if I keep "pushing it", it will come . . . but it usually does not *feel* good. I can *create* results but that is not my lesson here. The learning, for me, is to be in a place of *"allow"*. I know it sounds corny but it *feels* better. I would try to get into the "flow" of life instead of fighting the current by swimming against it. After the experiences of the last decade, I realized that I have choices on how I live this life and I decided that I wanted to be HAPPY and have FUN. Up until now, I had learned how to work hard, achieve goals, and create change. These skills would now serve me as "support" tools to help in this new, uncharted territory.

The main tool I now needed to look at was my own intuition. I realized it was **The Key** that I had bent and chipped by forcing it to fit into the lock on the door that *I wanted to open*. Intuition requires self-honesty and an element of trust. We are asked to trust that our key will open the doors that are meant for us to open. We must learn how to "fit" it properly! How to not jam it in and jiggle it around in order to "break in" to doors that are not for us, at least at this time. So I realized that I needed to re-define, re-learn, and *re-member* my Key. It has been a constant practice of checking in with what I call my "Essential Self" to keep the light shining on the next doorway of my life.

So if you are *feeling* lost, there is a lesson in being lost . . . an opportunity to discover something about yourself, your situation, and your life. Maybe your intuition is calling you to explore and step into uncharted territory, maybe it's your true path calling you, or simply gaining more clarity in your current inner life. That's all for you to answer . . . but I *trust* there is a reason the *feeling* is present . . . it may be a gift!

CHAPTER 2

ESSENTIAL SELF

The first step in this process of learning about your intuition is to realize that intuition is linked to authenticity. Intuition gives your authenticity a voice, it tells you when something is "off or not quite right". Intuition speaks to your authentic self through *feelings*. These feelings basically boil down to feeling "good" or "bad". So the big question is, how do you want to *really feel* in your life and why? The answers to these questions help to define *who you really are*, your authenticity. If you drill down a little deeper, you get to the more foundational question of "*what feelings are essential for you to be authentic?*"

The qualities of these feelings are what I call the Essential Self.

Essential Self is the foundation of authenticity.

The word "essential" is defined as what is "absolutely necessary and extremely important". The answers lead you to begin to recognize and develop the feelings of being comfortable in your own skin, relaxed, neutral, and *real*. This is unique to each individual. It ties into the answers to "what do you want?" and "what makes you happy?", but it's underneath all of that. It's the **WHY**. The "why's" help define WHO YOU ARE *essentially*. Why do you want ___? Why is that important to you? You need to answer these questions *first* in order to gain clarity about your own authenticity. If something *feels* important or "right", then that *feeling* is asking you to become more curious. What is important about the feeling? Why is *that* important? What **value** is the *why* pointing to? And therein lays an essential piece of YOU!

This is a process of distilling your feelings down to *what is essential for you to be aligned with what you value.*

It's a *feeling* that is linked to your values.

Intuition is *feeling your values.*

It can be pretty easy to identify certain feelings, especially positive ones like love, admiration, joy, and accomplishment. Some are a bit trickier; they show up in not-so-forward ways. It can feel like a "rub" or trigger. When a situation rubs you the wrong way, this is often the signpost that can cue you to take a closer look. It could show up as a feeling of defensiveness or judgement. It could be a physical feeling, a "gut response", and/or a shift in energy. The point is, that the rub is there . . .

what's that about? What I have learned to recognize is that when the "rub" appears, it is usually something that is rubbing up against one of the values that make up my Essential Self. This information helps you make decisions about how to choose your response, *aka response-ability*. This is a practice, a lifelong learning. Am I good at it yet all of the time? No way! Sometimes I really **suck** at it (remember the dream??). There are brief moments that I am **brilliant** at it. This is what I think life is all about, learning about ourselves so intimately and chipping away the rubble of our stories and unexamined beliefs, to uncover the beautiful sculpture that is our TRUE CREATION. That true creation is you, your authenticity, your Essential Self!

Let's take a closer look and dig in to the four main quadrants that make up your Essential Self, your heart, spirit, body, and mind by asking the questions, "**what is *essential* for you to *feel* authentic? And *why* are those feelings important to you?**"

The Heart:

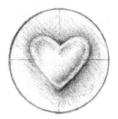

The heart is the place where your emotions originate from. Learning to recognize what is essential for your heart to *feel* is an extremely important part of learning about your unique authenticity.

- What is essential for you to *feel* when your heart feels it's best?
- How do you *want* to your heart to *feel*?
- Describe in detail the qualities of these heart- based feelings.
- Why are they important?
- What are the underlying values that these feelings describe?

For me, the feeling in my heart that lets me know I am in alignment with who I really am, offers me a sense of calmness, lightness and "space". It is an overall feeling of my heart being *relaxed*. It's kind of a "melting "feeling. My heart *feels* expansive and open, a place where possibilities lie.

Why is this important? The spacious relaxation of my heart speaks to my values of **being open, vulnerable, and real**. When those heart-based feelings are present, I am in alignment with true connection to my Essential Self, with another person, a situation, or decision. For me, these feelings are *essential* for true connection.

The Spirit:

The spirit is more of an *energetic* feeling than an emotional feeling. You can often identify it connected to a body focus and response. It lives in the body but is separate as well. I have learned that our life force energy runs through our body in a vertical line that goes from the top of our head to the soles of our feet. Visualizing the "chakras" of the body is a good start to understanding how this energy flows or gets stuck. I believe we all have our own unique vibration of energy to become aware of and learn to recognize how that vibration *feels* best to you and how those feelings are *essential* to be in alignment with your authentic self.

- How would you describe your energy level right now?
- Where in your body can you recognize it?

- How do *want* your energy to feel?
- Why do you want to feel that?
- What is "good" about it?
- Why is that important to you?
- What are the underlying values connected to those energetic feelings?

When I am most aligned with my authentic self, it is *essential* for me to *feel* grounded and balanced. The energy feels solid yet neutral and light, not "activated". The feeling/vibration lies in the core of my body (middle and lower abdomen). I also look to notice the sense of *relief* (more on this in the next chapter), an exhale, a feeling of gratitude, and inspiration (being in-spirit).

Why is this important? For me, the values that these energetic feelings represent are *essential* for feeling **balanced** energetically and having **gratitude** present in the situation, decision, or relationship. Gratitude is definitely an *essential* piece that I look for most often as a sign of authenticity. Gratitude for the sense that spirit (energy) is guiding me, gifting me, inspiring me or protecting me from the situation or "wrong" decision.

The Body:

The body communicates with us in physical ways, both internally and externally. Take a moment to think about these questions.

- What is essential for your body to feel its **best**?
- How do you *want* your body to feel?
- What is important about *that* and why?
- What are the values that are necessary your body to be aligned with your highest self?

Probably the biggest body feelings that I notice when I am in alignment with my values are relaxed shoulders, a sense of *feeling* light on my feet, lightless in general. I look to see if there is relaxation in my jaw and eyes, and examine what's going on with my skin. When I am out of alignment, my jaw muscles are tight and tense, my eyes are tired, and my skin gets hives and is itchy, the body signals of stress.

Why is this important? The feeling of a light, relaxed body points to the values of **self-care** and good **boundary setting** for myself and others. Choosing good nutrition and getting movement helps my body to stay agile and light. Movement also relieves my stress. All of this keeps me in alignment with ease and not dis-ease!

The Mind:

Ahh . . . the mind! This is where I believe we operate the most! The typically overworked part of our inner selves that at times can be a good tool but certainly not an objective tool! What is *essential* for your mind to be in alignment with your values/authentic self?

- How do you *want* your thoughts to *feel*?
- Describe the qualities of these thought related feelings in great detail.
- Why are these aspects of your thoughts important to you?
- What do you value from your mind when you are mentally aligned with feeling your best?

I am aligned with my authenticity when my mind is creative, open, and not in resistant thought. I value when my mind can turn off, as in meditation or simple daydreaming (I love the *feeling* of letting my mind drift away while watching the clouds or the wind moving the trees) and when I sleep well.

Why is this important? These *feeling* aspects of my mind point to the values of **peacefulness,** the ability to access **creativity,** and a **positive imagination.**

In order to define what is essential for you to authentic, let's go through the following questions and distill the answers down to what your values really are. Remember that these are descriptive words based on *feelings*. Let's get started!

When you feel the most aligned with *how you want your heart to feel,* let's explore the emotions and qualities of what is essential for your heart to feel it's very best!

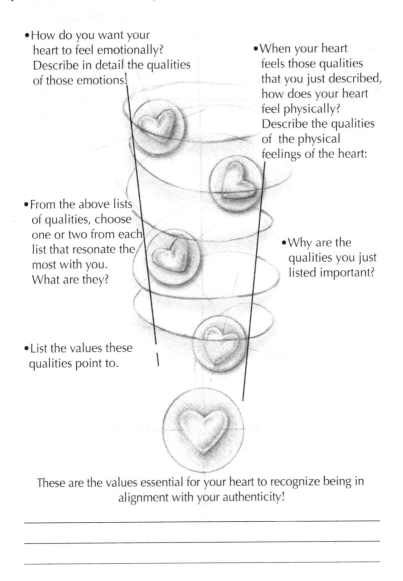

- How do you want your heart to feel emotionally? Describe in detail the qualities of those emotions!

- When your heart feels those qualities that you just described, how does your heart feel physically? Describe the qualities of the physical feelings of the heart:

- From the above lists of qualities, choose one or two from each list that resonate the most with you. What are they?

- Why are the qualities you just listed important?

- List the values these qualities point to.

These are the values essential for your heart to recognize being in alignment with your authenticity!

_____

_____

_____

31

Take a few minutes and try to recall a time in your life, a person you met, a movie you watched, or music you heard that caused to feel "inspired". Close your eyes for a moment and fully go into that memory. Notice all that is happening to you and around you in that moment.

Describe how that memory shifted your spirit, list the ways in detail how the inspiration "moved you".

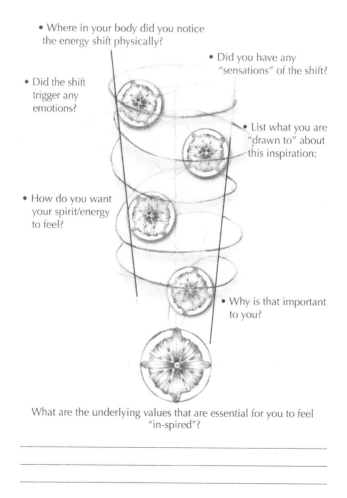

• Where in your body did you notice the energy shift physically?

• Did you have any "sensations" of the shift?

• Did the shift trigger any emotions?

• List what you are "drawn to" about this inspiration:

• How do you want your spirit/energy to feel?

• Why is that important to you?

What are the underlying values that are essential for you to feel "in-spired"?

_____

_____

_____

32

To determine what you value in your body, let's visualize your body at its best!

Take a few deep breaths and get present in this moment. Visualize a time when your body *felt* at its best. This could be from a time at any point of your life. Recall this time with as much detail as possible. You might want to close your eyes and *experience* this memory for a few minutes . . . describe in detail your memory:

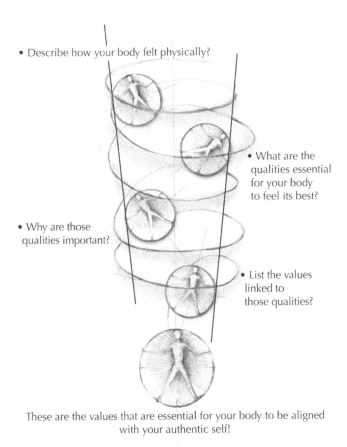

• Describe how your body felt physically?

• What are the qualities essential for your body to feel its best?

• Why are those qualities important?

• List the values linked to those qualities?

These are the values that are essential for your body to be aligned with your authentic self!

_____

_____

_____

In the quadrant of the mind, think about when your mind is operating in its best mode. This is different for everyone. Some people are drawn to a creative mind or a calm and focused mind; others prefer an active, multitasking mind. This is for you to determine what *feels* best to your mind!

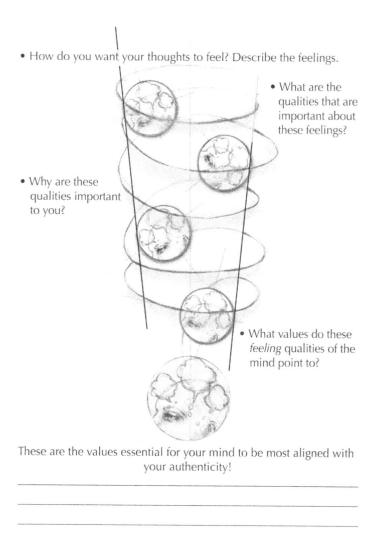

- How do you want your thoughts to feel? Describe the feelings.

- What are the qualities that are important about these feelings?

- Why are these qualities important to you?

- What values do these *feeling* qualities of the mind point to?

These are the values essential for your mind to be most aligned with your authenticity!

_____

_____

_____

List here the values for each quadrant that you have identified:

_____

_____   _____

_____

These are the values that are unique to you and comprise your own authenticity. I would suggest you write them down, commit them to memory, and fully step into *who you really are*!

Exploring through this process helps you to better understand *who you really are*, what is important to you, and why. This is your Essential Self, what is *essential* for you to be authentic and real. By dis-covering your authenticity, you clear away the clutter, the stories and beliefs that may not accurately define who you are, the *real* you. There is no one else that is uniquely you! You are the one and only!! Your life purpose is to be the full and beautiful expression of the uniqueness that is YOU!

The results of this exploration of what is *essential* for you to be authentic, is a sense of "remembering" who *you are*. There is a deep knowing and recognizing of self that is filled with self-love, happiness, and belonging. It makes sense when we look at the word "remember" . . . meaning to *re-member*, to put back together and reconnect the parts of yourself that got dis-connected by your life experiences, beliefs, and decisions that took you off track.

This is the basis of the Essential Self. What you define in these four quadrants will be the measure of your choices. The guideposts that lead you in the direction back toward the truth of *who you really are* and help you to make life choices that are aligned with the values of *what you really want*!

In the next chapter you will learn *how to discern* the ways that information presents itself to you in each quadrant. This information is vital to figuring out what is real and true for you within a situation or decision that you want or need to make. Let's get to it!

CHAPTER 3

HOLISTIC INTUITION; THE WAYS INTUITIVE INFORMATION COMMUNICATES WITH YOU

During the chapter of LOST, I began to look much deeper into my own intuition. Certainly it was there; I had ignored, rationalized, and otherwise turned my head on a lot of red flags that were trying to tell me something. It was hard to look at that truth and have compassion and empathy for myself. I realized that this was a pattern that I had done before, a pattern that led me way back to my childhood. I began to take a closer look at "defining" events in my life story and in each event, intuition played the lead role. Either I did not listen to it and allowed my mind to run the show, or I flat out betrayed my Essential Self by not setting healthy boundaries . . . the underlying piece that seemed flawed was my own guidance system, my intuition.

So I began to visualize a tool that could be used as a "filter" by developing my intuition in a way that was more holistic, a "checks and balances" if you will. The tool I decided to rebuild and refine was a key, specifically, *my key*. I would start with a "blank" key and intentionally carve into the "blade" of the key the same four quadrants of the heart, spirit, body and mind that I chose to discern and inform my Essential Self, my *feelings* that point to the *values* of Essential Self.

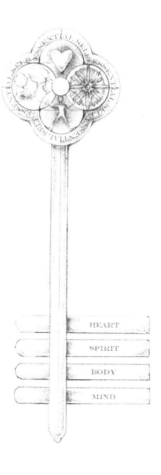

Your intuitive feelings, linked to your Essential Self values, are your *personal guidance system*. This is *your* key, your unique key that aligns with *who you really are*. Each of us has our own personal guidance system based on our unique intuitive *feelings*. Those feelings are guiding and communicating with us.

My own "a-ha" realization was, that through these defining moments in life, information was being expressed in order to help me make decisions. This was something larger than me, outside of self. **I realized I was being directed by a higher power through my intuition**. My lesson was to build faith and trust that something larger than my self was in play here. I also learned about self-honesty, self-empathy, and self-forgiveness about the choices I had made. In retrospect, I can see that they did not line up with what I *really* wanted before I had defined the values of my Essential Self. I had jammed my key into the lock of the DREAM, jiggled it around, and forced my way in! I knew I could no longer trust *my* plan, my previous operating mode of mainly my mind. I was being asked (*in a very real way*) to let go of control and trust a higher power to take the lead and show me the way through my intuition by learning to *feel my values*.

This learning is about defining and deciding to fully step into whatever FAITH means to you, whether you call it a "Higher Power" or "God" or "Allah" or the "Universe". Whatever *word* you use is who *you* are and that is perfect. I remember hearing Dr. Wayne Dyer describe the use of these controversial words as this: "Remember, you can't get *wet* from the word *water*" and we all have an understanding of what water is. It's not the word that is important here. It's what that word represents for each person and it's your choice to define your word, fill in the blank, and step fully into it. This is an important choice to make, even if you are not exactly sure of what you want to call it. It is a choice to step into faith, the faith that there is a larger purpose for your life and that you are being shown the way. I believe this Higher Power is *directing* our guidance system *through* our intuition and ultimately our direction in life if we can define, discern it, and trust it. For me, this word is God. I was raised Catholic but it is not the God I learned about there. It's the God that I have always known in my heart and have a deep and personal relationship with. It's a friendship. Most of the time I am filled with gratitude for this friendship, so thankful that I have this friend to lean on . . . sometimes I'm like "what the hell? Seriously? You have got to be kidding me right?" But regardless, it is a *true* friendship that remains a constant throughout my life. It helps me to recognize my strengths and understands my weaknesses. It is omnipresent and believes in me even when I make mistakes. It offers grace and forgiveness when I cross the line. It celebrates my successes and always offers *love* in every situation.

Like any relationship, it requires input, a give and take, understanding, compassion, gratitude, and asking for help when you need it. Most of all it takes SURRENDER, as in surrendering CONTROL (my plan) and learning to TRUST (the bigger plan).

However you experience or define this is a part of *your* journey. We each are in *our own unique relationship* . . . no judgement, no "right or wrong". It just is.

Let's take a look at the ways that *feelings* can present themselves as information to help guide you. In this order specifically, **heart**, **spirit**, **body** and **mind**, look at each one individually and then how they work interdependently to inform and guide your Essential Self when making a decision or trying to gain clarity in your life.

Heart

Firstly is the heart. This one, for me, is the riskiest one. For so long I had completely ignored the heart, so it has been a journey to reawaken and get familiar with this quadrant of myself. Heart based information is a vital part of who you are, who you love, and what you love. It is the measure of your emotions and encompasses your humanity through compassion and empathy. The heart holds the emotional palette of life's most wonderful and tragic experiences. It contains the spices that embolden or soften the events that transpire. The heart is a powerful informant that draws you in and has the strength to demolish, deconstruct, reform, and rebuild your life and the relationships in your life.

The **heart** speaks to you through emotion, some *feelings* could include:

- Feeling "moved" either in sadness or joy. The saying "_____ touches my heart" comes to mind
- A full heart/full heartedness
- A light heart/light heartedness
- A heavy heart
- A feeling of having a "hole" in your heart
- A feeling of having a broken heart/pain, sadness
- Feeling full of love or hate or nothing at all/empty heart
- A soft heart/ hard heart
- Warming feeling/a warm heart
- An icy feeling/a cold heart
- An expansive feeling/open hearted
- A constricted feeling/ closed hearted
- _____(add your own)

In my life story, my Essential Self learned early on to shut the door to my heart based feelings. I realize now how wise this was due to my life experiences. Closing the door on feelings was protecting me from immense pain from childhood experiences. The challenge was that the door closed early in life and I did not reopen it (or even realized it was closed) and develop the skills to recognize heart based wisdom for many years of my life. I disassociated from feeling my heart based emotions. It is a process to crack the hardened shell that keeps the heart encapsulated and enclosed, but the results are reawakening to a life filled with the colors of emotion, fullness, and true love. Cracking that veneer reveals vulnerability. Vulnerability to emotions, to being fully seen, to being hurt emotionally . . . and it also reveals vulnerability necessary for true connection, to feeling love, honest friendships, and authenticity. It requires courage to be vulnerable; courage to shed that hardened shell that we believe is protecting us from pain. The challenge is that the hardened veneer that we think is protecting us is also keeping us from fully feeling the multicolored experiences of living a life of joy, healthy relationships, fulfillment, and happiness. If you disconnect from the *pain* of life, you also disconnect from experiencing the *magic* of life. Be brave, peel off that hardened shell and courageously step into your life of *feeling*!

Spirit

The spirit is a little more familiar. I can clearly recognize where my *energy* is within certain situations but the learning was to not push through it or ignore it. The lesson is to discern it, question it, to follow its tracks to find its source. Where was this coming from? Is this me? Is it someone else? And if so, who? Spirit is asking us to surrender and trust. This is the quadrant where we connect to our faith. Spirit is directing us. It is our connection to something outside of self, larger than self, something that partners with self but is not solely self. This could be what some describe as Universal Spirit, Holy Spirit or Higher Power. Whatever term you choose, this is a place of *connection*, a sense of being connected to your *source*, being *in-spirit*.

Spirit feels like it's in control of the gas pedal in your car. You are in control of the steering. You can choose to turn right, left or stay the course. Spirit can move you slowly or very quickly. It can stop movement all together, leave you "idling" in your life. Checking in with spirit can be at times, easy to recognize. For example, think of a rollercoaster going fast. The experience could hold the *energy* of being uplifting, exciting, and free. Imagine you are in the front seat, hands up in the air wohooing with exhilaration! It could also be terrifying, super stressful, and feeling out of control, white knuckling the safety bar, eyes shut tight, and screaming out of fear! In this instance, it's easy to know where your *energy* is. Sometimes it is much more subtle; a tiny flame or a small *sense of* something. Searching for where your *energy* lies, in this case, may take some time in quiet reflection to access. It could take some practice to find it and become aware of it.

The **spirit** quadrant includes these energetic *feelings*:

- Increased or a boost of energy(lifting your spirit)
- Lethargy or decreased energy(low spirit)
- Motivation/compelling initiative
- A sense of being "pulled to"/drawn
- A sense of being "pushed to or away from"/driven
- Resistance (with someone, something, ideas)
- Connection (with someone, something, ideas)

- Flatness/disassociation
- Neutrality, groundedness
- Nervousness/anxiety/panic
- Relief/gratitude
- _____(add your own)

I'd like to take a moment to talk more about *relief.* Relief, I have discovered is a super underrated energetic feeling! In the experiences where I have felt *most* aligned with my Essential Self and my choices, the feeling of *relief* was very present. Sitting in the front row, raising its hand! This is an energy we all can relate to. It's the warming wash of *relief* that comes when the favorable test results come in, the feeling when a loved one in trouble gets help and real change, the resolution of a worry about something that gets resolved in a sudden and unexpected way. Imagine you look away for one moment and your child or your pet is gone. You panic, the energy is high in your chest area, constricting. Your heart is pounding in your chest. Your thoughts are running so fast you can't keep up. Your body is filled with adrenaline. Ten minutes later, you find your loved one sitting under a tree playing safely nearby . . . a HUGE sense of *relief* washes over you releasing those wonderful endorphins that then flood the body. The initial source of *relief* is energetic and linked to the value of gratitude. Then, your heart space is warm and full, your mind keeps saying "thank God" over and over again, your body relaxes and embraces your loved one, and slowly begins to find balance.

In this resolution moment, you are back into alignment with what is important to you, what you value. You are back in alignment with a piece of *what is essential* to you and your life. Yes, *relief* is under-rated and under-appreciated. It often goes unnoticed, unrecognized. I have found that this is such a huge signpost for me. *Relief* is what I am looking for and when it shows up, I pay attention. *Relief/gratitude* teaches me that I am energetically in alignment with my Essential Self, what is essential for me to be truly ME. It is a very good feeling.

Learning to notice where your energy lies within a situation or in making a decision is learning to *listen* to the ways we are being directed from our source.

Body

The quadrant of the body is even easier to recognize. Most of us know where in our bodies we hold stress and tension. We easily recognize the information we get from our "gut" feelings. I think the learning here is to *shift the paradigm* from our belief that "our bodies are simply physical" to "what is the information my body is giving me?" The body communicates with you all the time. It gives you feedback as to how you are living, how you respond to stress and relaxation, how you are nurturing or not nurturing yourself with nutrition and exercise. There are subtle and not so subtle messages from simple aches, pains, and sensations to disorders and disease. Look closely at those words . . . *Dis-order* and *dis-ease*. What aspects of your life are not "in order"? How can you shift and infuse "ease" into your life situation? This speaks to alignment or misalignment with your Essential Self and your current life situations on a physical level. Having had Stage 3 Breast Cancer myself, I often say that was one of the biggest gifts of my life. I will never forget one of my very first thoughts and *feelings* when I heard the words "you have cancer". I had a visceral, holistic sense of *relief*! The very same sense of relief I just spoke of in the quadrant of the Spirit. It surprised me, baffled me, and ultimately had me take a hard look at the choices I had made that kept me on the stressed out hamster wheel of life! I was given a *permission* slip to stop and take a break. It took the gift of cancer to shake my core, wake me up, and get *real* about how I want to LIVE! Cancer offered me the *opportunity* to get reacquainted and back into alignment with my Essential Self. What I was *feeling* from that sense of *relief* was the underlying value of gratitude for having this opportunity to open my eyes about how I was living.

Not to offend anyone here who is struggling with physical challenges but there is so much to learn about yourself and your life from these situations. Learning through dis-ease can be a daunting task but if you can find meaning and purpose for it then, whatever the outcome, it finds some sort of resolve in your life, some important meaning. *You are not your body. You are in relationship with your body.* How can you develop that relationship? What is your body telling you? Do you listen to your body? Our bodies are speaking to us, sometimes whispering, sometimes not so softly!!

Examples of information from the **body** include:

- "gut" responses like nausea, tightening, a "rock" in the pit of your stomach, a feeling of your stomach "falling or lifting", feeling "punched" in the stomach
- Tightening in jaw, throat, shoulders, hands, face . . . holding muscles tensely
- Body pains; sharp pain, dull aches, joint pain, headaches, congestion
- Physically unbalanced; vertigo, unsteady/clumsiness, dropping things, running into things
- Numbness
- A sense of feeling "lightness"
- A sense of feeling "heavy"
- Itching, skin rash
- Chills, goose bumps
- Heat; face, ears, heart, gut
- Dis-order
- Dis-ease
- _____(add you own)

I think we recognize body information because it commands our attention in such a *real time*, present way. How we listen to and assimilate the information can be expanded beyond the physical into a larger view of communication to help us move through life

48

with more ease. Imagine you and your body being friends with each other. How do you talk with or about your body? How do you nourish your body? In what ways do you nurture your body? In what ways do you diminish/shame your body? Or even flat out betray your body? How do you treat this friendship? Do you *really* listen to and respect this friend?

Mind

The mind . . . this is where I think most of us reside for the better part of our day! The mind is a wonderful, amazing, and imaginative place. It can rule our lives if we do not take time to examine the inner workings of our thoughts. The mind is not the same as the physical brain. Like the body, we are not our mind. The Essential Self as a whole has domain over the mind because we have the ability to choose our thoughts and perspectives. We can *change our minds*, how amazing is that? Even by changing our minds, by choosing a different belief or perspective, we can actually change the physical aspects of our brain! Pretty impressive stuff!

I often say that most of us walk around "from the neck up". We lean on the information from the mind for the majority of time. Most of us are also underdeveloped in accessing information from the other quadrants that make up the wholeness of the Essential Self.

The mind can also be tricky. If left unexamined, you may hold on to beliefs and perspectives that are not really *chosen* by you but more like *passed on* to you. You can take on belief systems from your families, society, and life experiences that if not questioned, may or may not be true for your Essential Self. It can be all too easy to fall into your "loop" of stories that you believe define who you are. This quadrant asks you to question those stories and decide if they are true. Many times we have been told stories about ourselves that we took in and believed. They have shaped our self-view and our world view. Sometimes we even boast about them! Sometimes we criticize ourselves with them. Things like: I've never been a good student, I just doesn't have what it takes, I have an Irish temper, I'm not good with math, I've always been stubborn, I've always been a joker, I'll never do___ good enough . . . the stories go on and on. The more we run the loop, the more we take them on as truth. They actually become *physical* connections in our brains that weave the fabric of our life experience!

We have all heard the saying "don't let your mind run away with you" in an emotionally charged situation. Those are good words of advice! It's no wonder that sayings like this one are passed on through time. They are words of wisdom and a reminder that Essential Self has the ability to choose thoughts and perspectives.

Information from the **mind** often reflects our own experiences/ life stories and can show up as:

- Perspectives/beliefs
- Judgments
- Knowledge/education
- Creativity/imagination
- Logical/conclusive thinking. Example: common sense/ decisive
- Illogical/inflated thinking. Example: paranoia/egoism
- Excessive/overthinking/worry
- Denial/ refusal to think about
- Acceptance
- Positive thoughts/optimism
- Negative thoughts/pessimism
- Obsessive/repetitive thoughts
- ____ (add your own)

I invite you to begin to notice your thoughts, your judgements, and your most hardened perspectives and ask your Essential Self the questions . . . "Is it true? Where did I learn this perspective? Did I choose it for my life view? Did I take on someone else's point of view? Do my thoughts, judgements, and perspectives reflect who I really am or choose to be?" Be very honest with yourself, notice what you realize, and **trust** that inner wisdom.

Within a decision or situation, information will present itself to you through these four quadrants of you Essential Self. The Key is used to examine what feelings are present and if they are aligned with *who you really are.*

Up until this point . . .

You have defined *who you really are* by defining your Essential Self values.

You have described and realized how those values *feel.*

You have explored the ways intuition can communicate with you.

Now, let's put all of this information together to see how we can develop better strategies for decision making and gaining clarity about our lives!

CHAPTER 4

CALL A MEETING; THE KEY TO UNLOCKING THE DOOR

Here is where we put all of this information together. Using holistic intuition, meaning your *whole self*, we can look at a decision, situation, or relationship through the lens of what we have defined as your Essential Self, what is essential for you to be aligned with *who you really are and what you really want*. This is a tool that you can use to discern which quadrants of your Essential Self are aligned and which are not through your intuitive *feelings*. It helps you gain clarity in a clouded situation when the mind overthinks or a situation that is too emotionally charged. A concept I learned from a friend of mine, co- facilitator and mentor, is a visual we can all relate to called, "call a meeting". It is very good at helping you gain clarity, make decisions, and choose responses to choices that arise in your life. Here is how it goes . . .

Imagine your kitchen table. Your table has four chairs around it. Now imagine these four quadrants of your Essential Self sitting around your table, your **heart, spirit, body, and mind**. Think of each part of *you* as your best friends, the closest confidants that you turn to when you need to talk things through. The trusted "people" you need for support and guidance that will give you honest feedback even when you really don't like the answers! You possess all of this guidance through these parts of your Essential Self.

Imagine a situation arises that triggers a *shift* in you, catches your attention. Think of that trigger simply as information and communication alerting your Essential Self through your holistic intuition. Information can be triggered first from any quadrant. Like a thought that comes to your mind or a physical feeling through the body, an emotion from your heart, or an energetic shift of some sort. That initial bit of information causes the other

The Key is Alignment

quadrants to react. Think of the "domino effect". One domino gets tipped and the chain reaction occurs.

Here is an example of how this situation this could look, imagine a situation with your closest friend. You had lunch with your friend and he told you about a problem he was having at work. It was really troubling to him and he was trying to decide whether to confront the issue or look for another job. He confided in you for your opinion and feedback on the situation. You listened, tried to ask him pertinent questions and gave your perspective. He was thankful and vowed to let you know how it works out. A couple of days later, you give your friend a call to find out how he's doing and follow up to see how the situation turned out. When he answers the phone, he's a little short and distant. He gives vague and quick details and then hurries off the phone. He seems to be upset or distracted in some way. Here comes the shift . . . your *mind* chimes in first and thinks "wow that was weird". Immediately you *feel* a shift in energy. It's unsettling, activated. Then the mind creates a steady stream of thoughts . . . maybe it's the conversation you had the other day when you gave some kind of feedback on his dilemma that he did not take well. Maybe you could have said it in a different way, is he mad at you? Down the rabbit hole your mind goes!

Then the *body* kicks in. You feel a "pit" in your stomach.

The "atmosphere" begins to feel un-easy.

Your energy (*spirit*) feels higher in your body; it rises to your chest/ neck area, and causes a sense of tightness in your throat.

Your *heart* feels a little shaky and you have the feeling of your heart "dropping".

Your *mind* creates a story that maybe you hurt his feelings and he is upset with you.

We've all been in situations like this and it's pretty amazing how fast this shift can happen. Within seconds, like getting hit by a big wave, your Essential Self gets flooded with information from the four quadrants of your intuition. It's no wonder that we find ourselves feeling overwhelmed. It's a lot of information all at once!

If you can, allow the information to flow freely and take note of what is showing up for you. Try to become an observer of the situation. You may be present enough to do this practice in the moment or choose to take it in and go through this process later. At any point in time, you can "**call a meeting**" with your Essential Self, your *heart, spirit, body* and *mind* **in this order.** Place the situation in the middle of your kitchen table in order to separate it and look at it from an outside viewpoint. Begin to ask some questions of your Essential Self that are about *your own internal state of being.* Not the story!

Here is a short and quickened example of how this meeting could look:

Questions you can ask the *heart* could be:

- How does my heart feel right now?
- What messages do I get from my heart?
- Does it feel hurt? Hardened? Tight? Neutral? Or nothing at all?
- Is it *true*?

Questions you can ask your *spirit* could be:

- Where is my energy in this situation?
- Is it elevated? Is it low?
- Did it shift?
- Is there resistance against/a push back?
- Is there motivation/a draw to find out more or "fix"?
- Is it *true*?

Questions you can ask the *body* could be:

- What is happening in my body right now?
- Is there tightness or tenseness?
- Is there pain?
- Am I relaxed physically?
- Is it appropriate to have this response?
- What is my body telling me?
- Is it *true*?

Questions you could ask the *mind* could be:

- Did I do any wrong?
- Did I offend this person?
- Did I not communicate well? Did I listen well?
- Was I kind, coming from a place of objective contribution or from my ego, layering on "my story"?
- Be VERY honest with yourself by asking the follow up question, is this *true*?

You may come to realize that the automatic response you experienced to your friend has no connection or alignment to you when you do an honest self-evaluation, meaning it was likely his "stuff" or that maybe you *did* play a part that your Essential Self is calling you to address. In either instance, you now have more information in order to choose a clearer response that *feels* aligned with your own truth, your values. This helps you to gain clarity and maintain integrity for yourself and your friend. There will be a settled feeling when you own your own truth about a situation, when you honor your Essential Self by listening and acting on the intuitive information that is being expressed to guide you.

Let's take a deeper dive into an example of making a decision. This example is about a big life change, a larger, life event decision! This could be career change, a relationship change, an important health change, a move to another country change . . . you get the picture. I think most of us can imagine a time in our lives when we had a larger decision to make or something that we wanted to change or required change. When you think about changing your life in some bigger way (fill in the blank), what is your pattern? What are your beliefs about change in general? Is change "hard"? Is change "exciting"? How do you *feel* about change?

Let's call a meeting and put "big change" in the middle of the table.

Starting with the heart:

- How does my heart feel about this change?
- Is there openness or a sense of tightness?
- What emotions show up around this change? List all emotions
- On a scale of 1-10 with 1 being full and open and 10 being closed and constricted, how do I rate my heart *feeling*?
- Does my heart feel full, excited, shaky, or flat?
- Ask each above question "is that true?" in order to get to the core of your answer and gain clarity. Don't stop asking questions until you feel complete and your heart is clear and settled with your answers.

Now we will ask your Spirit for information about this change:

- What happens to your energy level when you present the decision of changing this part of your life?
- Do you *feel* your energy increase? In what ways do you notice that?
- Do you have a decrease in energy? How does you energy *feel*? Describe it.
- Is there a sense of being "drawn to" or attracted to this change?
- Is there a sense of being "driven to" or a "should or have to" about this change?
- Do you feel a "connection" to this idea of changing?
- Do you experience nervous energy about changing?
- Does this change offer a sense of relief?
- Continue to ask each question again to find the most accurate description of the information Spirit is giving you through your own energetic sense.

How does the body chime in about this change?

- Do a "body scan" to see where there may be tension or tightness. Check in with your eyes, jaw, neck and shoulders. When you look at this change, do you notice any tension or "holding" in any of these areas? Ex: clenching your teeth, furrowed brow, pierced mouth, tightness in your throat, pain in neck muscles and shoulders.

- Are you holding your breath?
- Do you have pain anywhere in your body?
- Is your body relaxed as a whole?
- Do you feel grounded and balanced or not?
- Are you currently experiencing dis-ease or a dis-order? What information is your body giving you about that?
- Anything else? Keep digging . . .

What information does my mind have to offer (no shortage here!)?

- What are my beliefs about this change specifically?
- Does this change spark my imagination and creativity?
- Does it feel like the change offers a *feeling* of being "common sense"?
- Is my mind over-thinking or worrying?
- Are my thoughts mostly positive or mostly negative?
- Do I push my thoughts away (I don't want to think about it)?
- Does my mind feel calm and decisive about this change?
- BIG question to revisit with is **"is it true?"** The mind is the place we can so often get stuck in our stories and judgements that may or may not be true for us unless we examine them, and define them for ourselves!

The point of going through this meeting is to see where you are in alignment with the values you chose to be essential for how you *really want to feel* in your life. They are the foundation of who you are, the distilled down parts you defined as the essential pieces needed to be aligned with your own authenticity, your Essential Self. **Are those values present in each quadrant within this decision? Does this decision align with those values?**

This practice helps to create some space in any given situation in order to break the automatic responses that you experience that may or may not be aligned with the values that you want to *feel*. Calling a meeting with these parts of Essential Self, can aid in peeling off the layers of conditioning and getting down to what is *real* and *true* for you. It helps you to make better, more accurate, clear choices for your life and ultimately your happiness. It helps you to develop *true* responsibility. A more *true* "ability to respond", not simply re-act. To "re-act" is an action of the patterns that play out over and over in our lives that we are conditioned to. They may or may not be an accurate perspective. The practice is to ASK!

With this tool you can see if you are aligned with the *values* of who you essentially are in any given situation. Then make your choices based on *that* information.

Here are the steps to "Call a Meeting"

1. The situation, decision…arises
2. Call a meeting
3. Place the situation/decision in the center
4. *In this order*, go to each quadrant of your Essential Self and ask the question "how does my heart, spirit, body and mind *feel?*"
5. Where is there alignment with the values of Essential Self?
6. Where is there NOT alignment with the values of Essential Self?
7. Choose how to respond based on this holistic intuitive information
8. Surrender and trust the process!

This practice of "calling a meeting" with Essential Self can be used in all aspects of your life. Examples can include:

- Communication
- Choosing life paths/transition
- Decision making in all areas of life
- Relationship choices and challenges
- Life purpose and fulfillment
- Lifestyle choices
- Parenting styles
- Leadership/management styles
- Your own personal emotional, spiritual, physical, and mental state of being
  . . . The list is endless . . .

The four quadrants at the top of the key are the values of the Essential Self model. The four sections on the blade are the *feelings* that are linked to those values. Now let's use the imagery of a lock to represent a decision or life situation, specifically, the inner working mechanism of the lock. After going through the "call a meeting" process, does your key (Essential Self values) align with the inner workings of the lock in order to open the door? The alignment or misalignment can be found through your *feelings that represent your values.*

So with the Essential Self as your value system, you can use this intuitive information in any situation to see if you are in alignment with a decision you are trying to make and can offer clarity to that process. When you "call a meeting" with your Essential Self and the values that you have defined are present and all in alignment, you begin to trust that your guidance system is pointing you in the right direction. If any of these are not in agreement, you need to investigate and ask yourself to get honest about the answers. It could be that you have gone into your "story" about a situation or

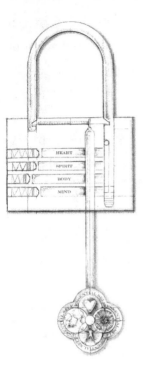

decision that you are trying to make. It could be a red flag that helps you define what *essential* piece is missing that you need to pay attention to. Maybe it's a simple matter of timing when one quadrant is out of alignment, asking you to wait awhile and see if it shifts. I can give the examples of my own answers but it's up to you to find yours. The good news is that you do not have to do it alone! I am always here to help if you can't find your way or get stuck within the process!

Sometimes it is clear when the key fits. It will be evident that how you feel about your situation or decision is in clear alignment with your Essential Self values. Often times this will be validation of what you already intuitively knew. Calling a meeting can be a great tool if you are seeking to find confirmation about your choices and to build confidence around your new process of decision making. Over time, this will help you cultivate a stronger sense of self- trust.

So what happens if your key does *not* fit? What do you do when there is not alignment? If you find yourself in the place where something feels "off" about a current decision or life situation, the space to look is within your Essential Self. Identify which quadrant or quadrants are out of alignment with your Essential Self values and ask yourself if there is a message that your intuition is trying to point out. You are being asked to take a closer look. Which quadrants are not in alignment? Does one stand out more than another? Have you *felt* this message before, is it familiar?

In my experience, a misalignment often shows up in to form of resistance. Resistance, for me first shows up in the quadrant of my mind. Misalignment with my mind will present itself with a sense of a "push back" to an idea, task, or decision. It's amazing when this happens because it sets off a chain reaction that extends and reaches the other three quadrants very quickly. The chain reaction within my Essential Self looks like this; first I feel the resistance as a "push back" or "block" in my mind which then evolves into thoughts of judgement. Then, my mind starts to circulate thoughts that create the feelings of anger and frustration in my heart as I grumble through the story. My spirit chimes in with an energetic shift that makes me want to "move away from", then comes the physical reaction in my body that feels like a sickening feeling in my stomach and body becomes heavy and sluggish. This happens so fast, but over time, I have been able to track its source and pattern so that now I can interrupt the chain reaction and catch it as soon as it shows up. The most important part of this process is to ask *"what message is this feeling offering me and what action is this feeling asking me to take?"* Is it asking me to slow down and examine the situation more deeply or be more proactive and move forward? Is this a yes? A no? Or a wait? As I have become aware of my own pattern, I have learned that this intuitive feeling of resistance is a message alerting me to slow down, explore further and trust there is a reason the feeling is present. I have learned to wait for clarity to present itself. Resistance, for me, typically means that I am going too quickly, that I am missing important clues, not seeing the whole picture.

During the experience of THE DREAM, the sense of resistance was "shouting out" loud and clear but I chose to rationalize it by labeling it "change". In retrospect, I can see it very clearly. I was being directed through this intuitive feeling. It was a message from my Higher Power to take a closer look. I simply did not *want* to listen and trust it. It takes vulnerability and courage to trust a feeling that you don't fully understand or just plain don't want to, but it is exactly what we are being asked to do when we learn to listen to and develop our intuition, our sixth sense instincts. Now I view resistance as a flashing light, a warning mechanism. Resistance still does not *feel* good and in the past, I would try to move away from it by pushing straight through it or ignoring it all together. Today, I look at resistance as my ally, *my advisor* within a situation or choice I am making. I am thankful to resistance for alerting me. It offers me the opportunity and space to slow down, take a closer look, and make a decision from that new perspective.

Information from the Universe can enter into you field of intuition through any quadrant depending on the situation or the patterns of how you experience life. It's like the air coming through a door or window in your home and creating a reaction within your interior environment. This could range from a big gust of wind that blows everything off the table to a gentle breeze that softly moves the curtains ever so slightly. The air could also be very still and peaceful or *too* still and stagnant! Intuitive messages enter through one quadrant initially and then cause the other quadrants to react.

We all have familiar patterns that are unique to who we are and our past experiences. It's interesting and good to know what your patterns are so that you can learn to recognize them more quickly, understand their messages and make choices that get yourself back into alignment faster.

What if it's just you?

What if there is no obvious reason for you to feel like you do? What if your feelings of misalignment do not have to do with a decision or life situation? What if your feelings can't be explained in that way? What if how you are feeling is *internal?* Or the even more loaded question of . . . what if it's just you? I say "loaded" because here is the space where you can jump into your own self-defeating patterns of thought, feeling, and action. Here is where the spotlight is on the many ways you can shame yourself, belittle yourself, and strengthen the patterns that keep you out of alignment with *who you really are* and *what you really want.* These are your habits, your conscious and/or unconscious patterns that may have been dominant, yet consistent in your life. The good news is that you have choices when you become aware of your patterns, notice when and how they initially show up, and decide to take action to realign yourself with your Essential Self values.

We all go through times when we feel "off, in a rut, in a funk . . ." but we are not really sure why. Maybe you feel depressed or anxious but there is no obvious external reason for those feelings to be there. I believe that when you are in this state of feeling unsettled, it is a message from your Higher Power to remind you of *who you really are, a* message to say "hey, pay attention!" These feelings are not *who you are*, not who you were created to be!" You may have fallen into the trap of your internal stories unconsciously; playing some old movie about yourself that is not in the obvious forefront of your mind. It could be an old memory that triggered this misalignment or a self-judgement that knocked you off balance. In situations like this, *you are our own trigger.* You can knock yourself off balance within any of the Essential Self quadrants by having unchecked thoughts or habits that create a shift or actions that are not in alignment with who you know you are *intuitively* and how you *really* want to feel.

In instances like this, it is important to have self-honesty coupled with compassion, understanding, and the most neutral self-view you can muster up. Taking your own inventory can be a daunting task but if you can practice becoming the observer outside of your own thoughts, actions, and feelings, you can begin to identify in which areas of your life that you can make new choices in order to guide yourself back towards the creation of your unique authenticity. Leading you back to who you were created to be in the first place. I believe that the more times you can catch yourself in misalignment, identify which quadrants of Essential Self are not *feeling* aligned, develop and most importantly *use* action tools to realign yourself, the better your life will feel!

Alignment and/or misalignment have to do with your *internal* state of being. Whether you feel confused about a choice you are trying to make or you simply find yourself in a "funk", or in a "rut" . . . your intuition is trying to tell you something. It is giving you a message that you are not in alignment with *who you really are*. I think it is important here to pause and take a few moments to explore the ways that misalignments show up for you. By identifying misaligned feelings in each quadrant, you become aware of them and will start to notice the patterns of how and when they show up in your life.

When you can identify how and when these reactions or misaligned patterns are happening, you have the ability to reach in and pull yourself out of the whirlpool of the situation and find ways to get yourself back into alignment with your Essential Self values. What are the tools and practices that you currently reach for when you want to *feel* better? What if you could use these tools **with the specific intention** to realign yourself back into the groove of your Essential Self *feelings/values*? The results of using these tools are to *intentionally* create the shifts that bring us back into alignment with how we *want to feel*. Let's brainstorm some possible ideas:

- Listening to music
- Playing music
- Reading an inspiring book
- Watching an uplifting movie
- Being in nature
- Engaging in prayer/meditation
- Exercising/sports
- Getting a massage/self-care
- Breathing exercises
- Yoga
- Journaling/writing
- Doodling, painting, art or creative projects
- Clearing out clutter/organizing
- Taking on a home project
- Doing an act of kindness for someone
- Connecting with friends and loved ones

- Cooking a delicious meal
- Dancing
- Singing
- Spending time with animals
- Taking intentional breaks from electronics/ TV/phone/ computer
- _____ Fill in the blank

These are things you do that make yourself feel better! They interrupt your patterns in a positive way. They are actions that you can take with the intention to shift your emotions, change your moods, lift you spirit, and feel good to your body and mind.

Let's go through the process of defining misalignments within yourself and then using your tools to realign yourself again. This process is called **Intentional Alignment**.

Calling a meeting with your self is a wonderful tool to use anytime! It can be so useful at times when you feel "out of sorts" or "off track" in order to see what quadrant or quadrants are not in alignment. By utilizing this check in, you can begin to clearly "see" where you are in any given moment or situation.

How does my heart *feel* right now? What emotions or quality of feelings are present?

Am I in alignment with my Essential Self values?

What are the intuitive messages that my heart is trying to tell me though these feelings?

In what ways can I intentionally align my heart with how I want to *feel*?

How does my spirit *feel*?

Where in my body and how does my internal energy present itself right now? Describe it

Am I in alignment with my Essential Self values?

What are the intuitive messages that my spirit is trying to tell me through these feelings?

In what ways can I intentionally align my spirit with how I want to *feel*?

How does my body *feel*? Do a quick body scan to see what is presenting itself in your body.

Is my body in alignment with my Essential Self values?

What are the intuitive messages that my body is trying to tell me through these feelings?

In what ways can I intentionally align my body with how I want to *feel*?

How does my mind *feel*? Describe the qualities of how your thoughts feel.

Are these qualities of my mind in alignment with your Essential Self values?

What are the intuitive messages that your mind is trying to tell me through these feelings?

In what ways can I intentionally align my mind with how I want to *feel*?

By getting this in-the-moment feedback from Essential Self, you can then make choices about how to move forward and/or explore ways to intentionally align yourself with *who you really are* and *what you really want*! Let's take a moment to list some actions you currently take and resonate with you to intentionally align yourself back with your Essential Self values. These are things you can do to make yourself feel better and more aligned to what is important to you. The results of these repeated and expanded actions affect the overall outcome of *who you really are* and *what you really want* in your life!

What are some positive actions you can take when you find yourself confused, angry, depressed, in a funk, anxious, not feeling like yourself, _____ (fill in the blank):

_____

_____

_____

_____

_____

_____

_____

_____

_____

_____

_____

_____

_____

By intentionally taking these types of realigning actions more often, you create the type of overall authentic life you want to live!

When you take some type of action with the intention to realign yourself, the same chain reaction happens within your Essential Self. *You create a change* in one quadrant and that change then affects the other quadrants as well! Once you align yourself again, you then can gain a more clear perspective on what is going on or a choice you are being directed to make.

I have started a practice of "calling a meeting" with my Essential Self at least two times a day to "see" where alignment is or not. I actually set-up reminders for this! This type of practice helps you to become more self-aware. It also creates a space for you to respond to how you *want* to feel. Within this space, you can use your tools to shift your feelings. It requires making a choice and taking action on your part, this builds the muscle of responsibility for your own internal state of being.

By utilizing this practice, you can get honest real time feedback which helps you to develop and gain clarity about your unique intuition, based on what you have defined as *your values,* not on your conditioning. It helps you to build holistic intuitive wisdom that is in tune with and connected to those values. **Note: you will make mistakes!!** The self-check-in practice teaches you discernment and refinement. It's a lifelong practice that you can learn and grow from through your experiences! After some time, you will learn to trust your intuition again (or maybe for the first time) and then all of this becomes more fluid, more automatic. You literally define and realign yourself with what is *real* for you, what is your *truth*. Anyone can do this in a matter of a minute or two. Remember, the key is to stay with *how do you feel within each quadrant of your Essential Self?* Not what your emotions are or what you think! Those are rabbit holes that could confuse you even more!

I believe that the more time you spend in alignment with your own amazing authenticity, the more you will actually *attract* the situations that offer positive relationships, a healthy body, financial freedom, and environments that are more suited to *who you really are and what you really want to feel.* An overall happier life! The more aligned you are, the more clear the messages and solutions can come through to you from God (my word). You are being directed through the guidance system of your *feelings*, your intuition.

While trying to see if your Key is a "fit", you may also be able to recognize patterns in your past that have not served you, like trying to unlock doors that were not your doors to unlock or misaligned decisions where you forced your key into the lock and broke your values against yourself! You may become aware of patterns that have kept you stuck. You can choose to shift these patterns but it requires some self-honesty, setting healthy boundaries, and the courage to step into *who you really are.* I believe it is *why you are here.* Your life's purpose is to be wholly, a full expression of your authenticity. BE YOU. You are a gift, a part of a bigger plan, a unique and beautiful creation.

Utilizing this intuitive tool, the Key can help you unlock new doors or lock old ones behind you! It can help you sort through confusing situations, help with decision making, find your true path and provide you with the freedom to define *who you really are* and *what you really want*!

CHAPTER 5

INTENTIONAL ALIGNMENT AND THE LAW OF ATTRACTION; THE REAL DEAL

Do you struggle with the Law of Attraction, the attraction and manifestation of what you *really want in your life?*

I believe in the Law of Attraction but have struggled to understand how it works for me. For years I have read about the many ideas of how to visualize what I want, create the feelings and actions as if I already have it, give thanks, and let it go. That all makes sense but it has not always worked that simply. I often *feel* like I'm "faking it" by reaching for feelings that are created within my imagination but do not *feel true* for my Essential Self. I understand the premise but have not been able to *feel* completely aligned with the process. I somehow feel "out of integrity". I get too attached to the outcome, my mind jumps in quickly and sets up expectations.

As soon as I shift into those expectations and start to look for evidence of what I desire becoming present . . . I feel like I shift into the *feelings* of "wanting or striving". Those feelings hold the expression of desperation for what I desire to show up and when it doesn't, I am disappointed and get a bit depressed. Expectations have knocked me out of alignment and *not* into attraction and manifestation. This is a pattern for me and has kept the illusive Law of Attraction misaligned with *what I really want*.

What if the Law of Attraction is personal? What if we each attract what we desire into our lives in our own unique way? It makes sense to me that if we are each unique creations, then we each have our own unique way to connect and attract our desires through the alignment with our Essential Self, which also places us in alignment with our Higher Power, our Creator. I am currently learning that the more you step into your own true authenticity and *intentionally* create alignment with your Essential Self; the rest will fall into place. Whoever created you knows your most inner desires, knows your highest potential, and wants you to live your best life! This all- knowing Creator already knows *who you really are* and *what you really want*. Your job is to re-member, re-connect and do your best to keep yourself in that alignment, *your* highest energetic vibration of your Essential Self and surrender the rest. You are always being directed either towards your Essential Self values or away from them through your *feelings, your authentic intuitive feelings.*

I remember a time years ago when we were looking to buy a home. When I look back, I can clearly see that I *attracted* this home into my reality *unconsciously*. I recall making a list of the qualities this home would offer (of course I did!). The list was in great but broad detail . . . It would be on a gravel road in the country, it would be totally private, it would immersed in nature with animals and birds, it would offer a sense of "softness" to my daily routine. It would be a great space to hold family gatherings and entertain friends. I would daydream and visualize what my mornings would be like there, listening to the birds, taking my coffee with me to the barn to start my daily chores with my horses (that I did not have yet). I would imagine enjoying the sunshine and the feeling a soft breeze touching my face. I did this without really "setting an intention" for it. I *just knew what I wanted it to be like* and would make my lists and daydream about it on a level of "going fully into it" in a mental, physical, spiritual, and heart- driven way. I was not *aware* that I was attracting this into my life in any way.

Over a few weeks, I went with our realtor to look at properties out in the country. One particular day, a house popped up in an area that I had not considered. The price was considerably lower than it should have been which is why I had not looked into this area in the first place. I wondered why and what was wrong with it? There were no photos included in the listing and it was not described as what I was looking for particularly but *something in my intuition* directed me to check it out. It was a *small* feeling and I did not think about too much. I just figured "why not?" I asked the realtor if we could just swing by to take a quick look as we headed out further into the countryside. It was right outside of town in an area that I was really familiar with, an area that I spent a lot of time in during my youth. We drove along and as we turned onto the road the house was located on, the road shifted from asphalt to gravel, we got to the driveway and drove up. The house did not look like much on the outside, it was kind of "blah" but we thought we'd go in and take a look since we were already there. As we walked through the front door, I *knew in that very moment* that this was the home I was looking for! It was as if someone suddenly knocked all the pieces right into place, right into alignment with my list and even though it did not "look" like it, it *felt* like it. The "bones" and layout of this house immediately *felt right* to me. The décor . . . not so much! It had purple carpet, ugly wallpaper in the bathrooms, and the walls were an institutional gray . . . flat out ugly! But it was open, it had big windows that connected you to the nature outside, it was completely private, you could not even see any of the neighbors' homes, it had an old barn and a stunning deck area. It was exactly the aspects of what I had daydreamed about! I called my husband, he came out right away and felt the exact same way, walking through the door, and without looking any further he said "this is it". We made an offer on the spot and got the house! It *felt* like a gift. It was a gift. Without knowing what was lying ahead, it ultimately offered a space that held our values of having our family and friends there, provided a place for my parents to live until the end of their lives. It gave me the experience of having my horses (a dream I had since I was a child), and a beautiful place to be during the challenges of going through cancer treatments.

I realize now that I *attracted* this gift into my life through the process of defining and imagining how it would *feel* to have it. Not what it looked like, where it was, when it would show up, how much it would cost . . . I certainly did not envision purple carpet!!

I recognize that this alignment was connected to and manifested through the quadrant of my heart. The feelings and visualizations originated from my heartfelt desires, and then quickly entered my spirit in the way of feeling relief/ gratitude and feeling grounded. My mind created the list and allowed me to daydream about it in a creative, positive way, not in a "striving" way. My body connected to a feeling of being relaxed and in ease. Yes, in retrospect and completely unaware . . . I was in perfect alignment with my Essential Self. I now am realizing that I was using the Law of Attraction without knowing it!

So here is what I am beginning to understand . . . that if we can define and connect to the *feelings of our desires* in a "broad" sense and if they are in alignment with our Essential Self values, then we can *attract* those desires into our reality. **This part is really important, we have to let go of the "who, what, when, where, or how" these desires show up!**

Now, I intentionally use the word "desire" vs. "want". As in "what do I desire vs what do I want?"

The root of the word "desire" is from the Latin "desiderare" meaning "to long for, demand, expect" and from the original sense of the word and my personal favorite *"from the stars"* or to *"await what the stars will bring"*. That's powerful! This holds a feeling of excitement and of expectant anticipation. It *feels* open to possibilities, positive, and broad. A confident knowing and trusting that at the right time it *will* show up. There is sureness about it. It does not say await what the stars *might* bring. It says *will* bring!

The root of the word "want" dates back to the Norse meaning of "to lack, to want" or "to feel the need of". That's a totally different feeling! This *feels* like striving for something to come into our lives, hoping it will but not feeling confident or having trust that it will. Like "maybe it will, I hope so". It *feels* more uncertain, narrow, and less than optimistic.

So if we are to utilize the Law of Attraction by accessing our *feelings* to attract something, it seems much better to fall into the abundant feeling of *desire* vs the scarcity feeling of *want*!

This is a **huge revelation** to me. For so long as I tried to understand and practice this Law of Attraction, I had been coming from a place of want . . . as in I want to win the lottery, I want a new chapter in my life, I want a NEW DREAM. But again, it comes back to and is connected to *why*. *Why* do I want this, what are the values connected to the *whys*? And most recently . . . are those *wants* aligned with *most valued feelings* within what I have defined as my Essential Self? Are they what I *really* want? What I *desire*?

The BIG A-HA! The Law of Attraction is connected to alignment or misalignment with your Essential Self values! Holy crap, the

BIG lightbulb just lit up! A big download from the universe that connected the dots and is now asking me to share this with you!!

The Real Deal

So just like we used the "call a meeting" tool to make decisions about a situation or to gain clarity about ourselves, we can use it as well to check in about what desires we would like to attract into our lives. My desires are likely no different than most of yours in a broad sense. I desire a strong connection to God, loving relationships, financial freedom, a healthy body, and a larger sense of purpose. How these desires *feel* to each of us as individuals is what sets up our unique authenticity. If I place my desire in the center of my table and have a conversation with each quadrant of my Essential Self, I can begin to gain clarity on how they each *feel* to me and if I am clear about what I am *really* wanting to attract into my life, my heart's desires.

We all know the saying "be careful what you wish for". I think this speaks to attracting something into your reality that is not best aligned with *who you really are*. I can see this with my life experience of the DREAM. On the surface, it held many of the desires I wanted to attract into my life but did not encompass the broader picture entirely. It offered a new place to live, a sense of purpose, and building relationships with others. It did **not** hold my desire to have strong family relationships, financial freedom and an overall sense of healthy boundaries and self-care. There were missing pieces to this dream and all of the intuitive signs that were directing me, I ignored. It was, in the broader sense, the BIG CHANGE that I was wanting but did not hold the *all of the feelings* that my Essential Self *desired* most. It was a "be careful what you wish for" scenario and I certainly got it!

Then, on the flipside is the saying" Sometimes *not* getting what you want is a wonderful stroke of luck!" We've all experienced this one. This is when you *think* we really want something to happen and it does not happen. In retrospect, you can look back and say "thank God that did not happen!" In this instance, you may have only wanted something from one particular quadrant but it may not have been aligned with *all* of your Essential Self values so it was not attracted into your life. It could be like wanting to marry a certain person, wanting a new job, wanting something about yourself to be different than it is. In cases like these, you can look back and "see" that _____ (fill in the blank) was not in your overall best interest. It could have seemed like a "fix" at the time but not in the broader view of what you desire to attract into your *whole* life, not just one aspect of your life. Remember each aspect affects the whole. One piece of the puzzle does not complete the entire picture. That was the mistake I made with the DREAM. Now I see it clearly and have learned so much from this experience.

The key is to reframe and get *very clear* about what you desire to attract into our lives from a panoramic view, call a meeting and see if how each quadrant feels about it. Does what you desire align with your Essential Self values? Does it offer a "yes" to those values and does it fit into the larger picture and include the other aspects of your life that you envision? Are there missing pieces? Think of it like a puzzle, a puzzle of your life.

I now have the desire for a new dream that I have named the REAL DEAL. I can clearly see that the DREAM that led me into the wilderness of LOST has revealed to me what those missing pieces were and now I have so much more clarity because I am coming from a place of heart-based desires, values, and authenticity instead of attracting from a place of *want* and striving to create change. I simply *did not want to listen* to the information my intuition was trying to tell me. I wanted what I wanted, a big change. The good part is that I learned so much from the experience and now have the opportunity to step into this space of attraction with clear intention for ALL that I desire and not just parts of it.

So here's the REAL DEAL . . . A New Dream . . . A New Opportunity

What my heart *desires* to attract into my life is:

- A new opportunity that keeps me connected to my family and being connected with my husband. Something my husband and I are doing together.
- Financial freedom so that I can help others and elevate my family, friends and the world in general.

- A larger life purpose that leaves a legacy for my grandchildren and future generations to expand on.
- A new place to call home that offers my desires to be in nature with privacy, light and openness.

Are my desires aligned with my Essential Self values? *Why* do I desire this? How does each of these desires *feel*?

My personal Essential Self values are:

 I value my heart feeling relaxed, expansive, open, vulnerable, and real

 I value my spirit feeling relief/gratitude, balanced, grounded and inspired

 I value my body feeling light, healthy, and relaxed, and the values of self-care and good boundary setting

 I value my mind feeling creative with positive imagination, not resistant, day dreaming, night dreaming, and good sleep

When I look at my desire to attract the REAL DEAL into my reality, I can check in to see if all of those aspects of my desire offer me the feelings that are my Essential Self values.

I can clearly see that my desire IS in alignment so I can begin to surrender the "who, what, when, where and how" and have a confident knowing that my desire, *offered from the stars*, **will** come into my life.

My responsibility is to keep my feelings aligned with my Essential Self values. This is where I will have a vibrational match to attract what I desire into my life. If it *feels* real, meaning authentic, then it's the REAL DEAL. These are not feelings that I have to muster up and reach for or feelings that I have to reason with and justify. These are the feelings of *who I really am*.

When my unique desires, *what I really want* and how they *feel* are aligned with *who I really am* . . . there is an aligned match.

It is a discipline to not go any further than that! What I mean by this is that you can knock yourself out of alignment if you get into the details of what you desire. Things like what it may look like, giving it a timeline to arrive or any specific way it will manifest. When you step into the space of "who, what, when, where, or how" you step *out* of surrender, allow and trust into a place of **control**. Those are external factors are not in your control. The parts that *are* in your control are held within the tools that help you align with your feelings, your self-care practices spiritually and physically and monitoring your thoughts in order to stay aligned with *who you really are*. For me, the biggest trap to manifestation has been the attachment the "when", to the timing. If you get attached to when your desire might manifest, you move out of a place of allow and into a place of mistrust. Mistrusting that the "stars will bring". This will shift you away from alignment. This is a really important piece of realizing and becoming clear on your faith. Do your best to gain clarity on "in whom or what" you are placing this trust. Again, for me, it's God but connect to whatever term resonates with your Essential Self. Maybe it's a word or name that *feels* best to you. I believe it does not matter what you call it . . . it just is what it is. When the desires show up, it is then your choice to make a decision to take action or not. The external is up to God. The internal is up to you.

Alignment = Attraction

So what do you do now?

I put together what I call an "Intention Board". It's like a vision board with the focus on alignment with your Essential Self values. In the vision boards I have done in the past, I have placed pictures, words, drawings, quotes . . . of what I would like to attract into my life. It has been interesting because some of the things on my vision board have come to me over the years, many of them actually, but not all. So I am looking back to see where I may have not been clear or *really* had alignment with what I thought I wanted to attract into my life and *why*, the "why's" point to my

Essential Self values. Now, I place my Essential Self values in the center to remind me to check in with my desires to see if they match up with *who I really am*. Do these desires hold *all* of the values that I listed for my Essential Self? Do they align with my unique authenticity? Do they interconnect with the whole picture and not just one piece?

This is a helpful tool to get yourself aligned with what you *desire* by aligning with *who you really are*. It's a place to daydream, visualize, and meditate. A place to focus on when you feel out of sorts in order to help get you back on track and also a place to come with gratitude when you feel most aligned and have experienced something manifesting into your life!

Remember, the key is to stay in the panoramic view of your heart's desires, not down into the details of the specific ways they could look or the ways they might show up. Try to not get attached to the "who, what, when, where, or how's" of it. Stay above all of that and *allow* the Universe to deliver without those strings attached. The strings are what pull you out of alignment.

The 6 step process to defining your **D.E.S.I.R.E.** to place on your Intention Board is (see illustration on page 92):

Let's explore each step individually.

D. Desires. On a separate piece of paper, start with a list of what your heart desires to attract into your life. Try not to "think" about this, just allow the desires to flow through your heart and jot them down. Remember to focus on what your heart *really wants*, your true desires. Brainstorm all of ways your life will be affected by your desires and how they will *feel* to you when you have them.

E. Essential Self values- Do your desires align with *who you really are*? Do they offer the feelings that align with your Essential Self values? Place your Essential Self values in the center of your intention board. Examine each of your desires from your list and see if they align with your values in order to gain clarity about *what you really want* to attract into your life. You can do this by asking the question "why do I want this in my life? How will I *feel* when I have it?" Once you are clear on your desires, write your descriptive words (in pencil) in the area of your intention board marked "desires" in the quadrant you feel is the most appropriate.

S. Essential Self values- Do your desires align with each other? Do they "fit" together in the larger view of the life you want to attract that is aligned with your Essential Self values? Are any pieces missing? This is the space where you can begin to look at the whole picture to see if any desires are conflicting with each other or if there are any pieces missing. You may also gain more clarity about the desires you have chosen and revise, remove or add more accurate descriptive words. Do your desires interconnect to align with the bigger picture of your life?

I. Intention. Place your **Intention** on the board with representations of what your desires will attract into your reality. Get creative here! Find pictures, draw or doodle illustrations, find feeling words, quotes, images that represent your desires, and add them to your intention board in the area of desires. Step back and take a broader view of the life you want to attract. Do you need to adjust or rearrange anything? Do you need to add or remove anything? Remember, you can always come back to this at any time and adjust as life changes or you gain more clarity. This is a fluid intention board that ebbs and flows with the guidance and information from your intuition and Higher Power. Listen to your holistic intuition to guide you through your *feelings*. Place your intentions in the quadrant area of the board that feel like they belong there remembering that they are all interconnected like puzzle pieces and can be move around at any time. There is no "right or wrong" here!

R. Relinquish control as in, surrender it, and let it go. Turn it over to your Higher Power. It is important here to advise you to not get stuck in the creative process. Develop your intention board to a place that *feels* really good to you and STOP. You can revisit on occasion if you want to update or revise but staying "in it" speaks to *not* surrendering it to the universe and holding your desires in the grip of your hand instead of releasing and attracting them into your reality.

E. Exhibit faith and trust that it is on its way! *Exhibit is a verb that means to manifest* or deliberately display, it is an *action word* that suggests to me that if we take action to intentionally align ourselves with *who we really are* and *what we really want* . . . it will manifest!

That's it! Leave the rest alone, walk away and go about your day without obsessively thinking/wanting it. Learn to trust that the stars *will* deliver!

You can choose to name your intention board as I named mine "the Real Deal" or not. Do what feels best to you, makes your heart smile when you connect to it. That's the key. When you want to attract something into your life, it's imperative that it makes you feel good every time you think of it!

You can place your **Intentional Alignment Tools** along the outside edge of your board to remind you of the actions you can take when you are out of alignment. They represent the external actions that *intentionally* put you back into alignment with your how the desires you want to attract make you *feel* and into alignment with your Essential Self values. Here is where you intentionally create the feelings to attract *what you really want* into your life. Remember that's your part of the process. The rest is up to your Higher Power to put together the "who, what, when, where, and how" of it!

Here is what the intention board looks like followed by an example of what my "Real Deal" intention board looks like completed so you get the idea.

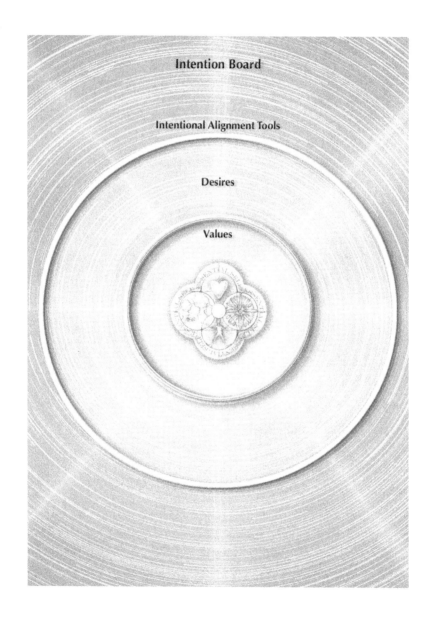

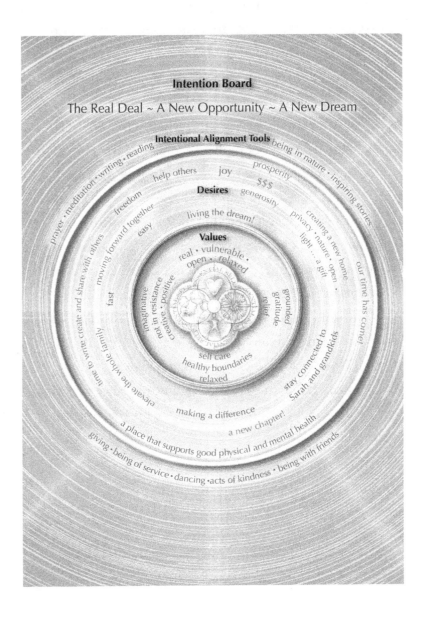

I usually focus on my Intention Board in the morning with my coffee and then again before I go to sleep. When I find myself restless or in a funk, I can return to it throughout the day to keep myself on track. The Intention Board connects me to my desires; it makes me smile every time I look at it. It invokes good feelings and helps bring me back in line with *who I really am* and *what I really want*. It elevates me to rise above the place of "want" and into a higher vibration of desire. For me, this process resonates so strongly with *who I am* that I trust this is *my* process. I share it with you in case you have not fully been able to connect with the Law of Attraction in your life. If this information resonates with you, give it a go and have fun with it! This is information that I am receiving and learning about "real time" and I *feel very much* directed to share with you now. I feel like I just was given my very own special key that will unlock the ancient door to attraction and manifestation in my life! I believe this information is for you too, for you to see the path that leads to your very own unique door. The path that leads to toward your heart's desires and the life you *really want* to live . . . the life you were uniquely created for!

CHAPTER 6

FINDING YOUR PATH

Finding your path in any decision or in setting intentions is simply finding alignment with what you value. "Calling a meeting" is an **external** assessment tool that you can pull out of any given situation to take a larger view at what is true for you. The four quadrants of your intuition are your **internal** guidance system that informs "your key" of whether you are in alignment with your values, through the observation of *feelings* and not just thoughts or emotions. If you are in alignment with your values, the key will fit and you can choose to open that door. The choice is yours to take that action or not.

So with your Essential Self intact and your Key in your pocket, you can go about your life with the confidence of authenticity. Use your Key to look for alignment. Sometimes you will be aligned, sometimes you won't. Over time, the results of creating a pattern of this "self-check-in" will become a deeper and more fluid experience of trusting your intuition and making choices that offer you a more fulfilling life experience. So many times I have heard people talk about their "life purpose". I've talked about it too! But what I have come to believe is that it is simple (sometimes not so easy!). You are simply meant to *be fully you* by finding alignment with yourself through the guidance and connectivity to your source. This source, what I call God, "speaks" to you through your holistic intuition. You are being *directed* in this experience we call *life*.

The results of defining Essential Self and developing your intuition can help you to view your life through a new lens or perspective. Holistic intuition infuses information and guides you in decision making, choices in relationships, and career paths. Defining your values also helps you to learn to set better boundaries in relationship with self and others. You become better parents, partners, and co-workers because you now have a clear vision and knowledge of *who you really are* and *what you really want*, not just the reactive thought patterns or emotions to a situation. When you have this level of relationship with and understanding of your own authenticity, all of your old "stories" that you have defined you in the past can then be transformed into "life experiences". Experiences to learn from and grow from. You have become the alchemist, turning everyday metals into gold! You no longer see through the lens of those stories. You are now **empowered** by them because you have learned the lessons they had to teach you about YOU! They are now your allies, your new tools instead of your faults and past mistakes. Through these processes, you then develop an unshakable self-confidence, a strong sense of integrity, independence, and interdependence. When you no longer allow just your thoughts and/or emotions to run your life, you reach a higher level of *intuitive development* and maturity . . . a step further than just emotional maturity and a more solid foundation for *intuitive responsibility*, the ability to respond based on more holistic (heart, spirit, body, mind) information from your Essential Self, your values, your intuition, and ultimately your connection and relationship with what you define as your Higher Power.

It's a practice really. A practice that takes practice! Sometimes we will get it right, learn to "see" red flags, trust them, and act on them. Other times we will doubt ourselves, rationalize, and justify our choices. Nobody is perfect. We will continue to make mistakes. But through all of this, we will celebrate our good choices and have the opportunity to learn from our mistakes. Learning from mistakes *deeply* informs us about what essential pieces we missed or didn't even realize were there! Your life is about recognizing your uniqueness and learning to genuinely like and be comfortable in "your own skin". You are a unique being inside and out. You possess your own unique physical body, feelings, perspectives, and preferences. No two people are exactly alike! That is pretty amazing when you stop to think about it for a while. My wish is for you to re-member your own authenticity as the incredible, one of a kind creation that *you really are*. I pray you find *your way* and en-joy *your life*!!

Always with love…

ACKNOWLEDGEMENTS

I'd like to first and foremost thank my husband Kriss for his never ending support and patience through the process of writing this book. This has been quite a journey for us both and here we are . . . hand in hand, my very best friend who has encouraged me every step of the way. Thank you so much Kriss for "getting me"!!

To my sister who did all of my illustrations that brought the teaching of this material to life, you are such a treasure in my life! Your creative talents are outstanding and capture to perfection what my mind's eye visualized. This book would be incomplete without your drawings that so aptly express what I am trying to say.

To my friends and family who have supported me, given me honest feedback and had to listen to the endless conversations that allowed me to process what I was trying to convey. Thank you for your patience and kindness! You are a part of this book as well and I have gratitude for you all being a part of my life journey.

Ultimately my thanks go to God for the inspiration, direction and lessons you've been trying to show me for so long. This began with you and I feel it is from you that this information is shared. This is your book written through me. Huge gratitude.

ABOUT THE AUTHOR

Cris is a Professional Life Coach, writer, author, inspirational speaker and educator. She also has many years of experience in the field of Equine Assisted Learning and has authored and facilitated a variety of custom programs and retreats in the areas of personal growth, leadership and self-awareness.

Cris is an entrepreneur, owning her own businesses since 1988. Her life experiences include learning through childhood trauma, single parenting, learning through breast cancer, supporting others in addiction recovery, caring for aging parents and the very profound and personal lessons that these events can offer us. She has spent her life serving others and was featured as an honored guest on the Oprah Show.

AND, who Cris IS, is not only about what she has done in her life, not solely focused on achievements and successes. She is, in fact the sum of all of the lessons learned from those experiences. She is a deeply caring, easy to talk to, down to earth personality, void of pretense.

Cris is the real deal, authentic, a good listener and possesses a good sense of humor. She is easy to be around. So as the above list of roles is important to know, more importantly is to get to know the person!

Cris's passion and purpose in life is to love God and help others. Simple as that.

Please visit www.cmlindsay.com for more information.

ABOUT THE ILLUSTRATOR

Carmen Lindsay has worked for over twenty-five years as a professional artist, graphic artist and designer. Her range of experience includes working as a type setter, production artist, graphic artist, art director, illustrator, and designer. She has broadened her creative talents to now include silversmithing and is working as a freelance graphic artist, fine artist and illustrator.

Carmen has studied advanced modalities of art at the nationally recognized Corcoran Museum of Art and internationally under well-known botanical artist, Pandora Sellars. Carmen has had a lifelong passion for art and a commitment to continue expanding, refining, and becoming a master in her vocation.

She has raised three wonderful children and is living in California and has a deep appreciation for nature and wild life...

CPSIA information can be obtained
at www.ICGtesting.com
Printed in the USA
BVHW030348210720
584204BV00005BC/17/J